PSALM 7

PSALM 7

A Commentary

TRAVIS C. MALLETT

VORSTOßEN
ACADEMIC PRESS

VORSTOßEN
ACADEMIC PRESS

First published in 2021 by Vorstoßen Academic Press
www.vorstossen.com

Publisher's Cataloging-in-Publication Data

Names: Mallett, Travis C., author.
Title: Psalm 7 : a commentary / Travis C. Mallett.
Description: Includes bibliographical references and index. | Pullman, WA: Vorstoßen Academic Press, 2021.
Identifiers: LCCN: 2020914432 | ISBN: 978-1-953516-00-8 (Hardcover) | 978-1-953516-01-5 (pbk.) | 978-1-953516-02-2 (ebook) | 978-1-953516-03-9 (pdf) | 978-1-953516-04-6 (audiobook) | 978-1-953516-05-3 (audiobook)
Subjects: LCSH Bible. Psalms—Criticism, interpretation, etc. | Bible. Psalms, VII—Criticism, interpretation, etc. | BISAC RELIGION / Biblical Criticism & Interpretation / Old Testament | RELIGION / Biblical Criticism & Interpretation / Old Testament / Poetry & Wisdom Literature | RELIGION / Biblical Studies / Old Testament / General | RELIGION / Biblical Commentary / Old Testament / Poetry & Wisdom Literature
Classification: LCC BS1450.7th .M35 2020 | DDC 242–dc23

Library of Congress Control Number: 2020914432

Proofreader and copy editor: Kevin O'Malley

Cover design by Travis Mallett with Inkscape 1.02 (Copyright © 2021 Inkscape Developers). Cover image credit: iStock.com/Grafikactiva

Typeset by Travis Mallett in LATEX using Texmaker (Copyright © 2003–2021 by Pascal Brachet)

Version 1 | ID 6dvgye

Printed in the United States of America
on acid-free paper.

∞

CONTENTS

PREFACE

This commentary is the outgrowth of research conducted while composing a contemporary art musical setting of Psalm 7.[1] The development of this commentary provided significant guidance for the musical elements in the composition to either directly reference the text or reinforce a coherent musical structure. For example, the instrumentation is divided into three parts corresponding with the three characters represented in the text of Psalm 7—the psalmist, the accuser (or Cush, a Benjaminite), and the Lord.

The bulk of the musical structure of the composition is defined by numerological devices in accordance with the structure and historical context of the text. Psalm 7 was originally understood in reference to a specific historical event that is now unknown. The commentary pays close attention to the historical background of the text and presents the major theories that have been proposed. As this commentary explains, Psalm 7 has the unique property of being both the seventh psalm as well as using various names for God seven times. Following these numerological observations, serialism was used for generating musical materials.

The material consists of a tone row, eight notes long (based on the division of the text: seven sections with a concluding hymn of praise). This row drives both the macro- and micro-structures of the music as shown in Fig. 1. Psalm 7 was labeled a *shiggaion*, a term that gives the notion of a wandering, erratic poetical form. The tone row itself is constructed to illustrate this: [1 4 2 9 5 3 6 7]. This row, in fact, does *not* make a good melody in the traditional

---

[1] Mallett, Travis C. *Psalm 7*, Opus 16 (2014). [Score] Pullman, WA: Travis Mallett, 2014

sense defined by the masters of counterpoint. Instead, it has little form, direction, or melodic arch in accordance with the implications of the term *shiggaion* and the nature and structure of the text. For example, the direction of the intervals are [↑ ↓ ↑ ↓ ↓ ↑ ↑]. This alternation produces a lack of direction and gives the sense of wandering around, per the connotations of the term *shiggaion* and the nature of the text in Psalm 7 and Habakkuk 3, as explained more fully in this commentary.

Listeners of the musical composition are encouraged to study both the text of Psalm 7 using this commentary and the composition itself. A deep understanding of the text can be drawn from the music through study and repeated hearings with a spirit that wishes to seek the face of God and understand His truths. Scholars of the Old Testament will also find this commentary useful as it consolidates much of what has been said in the past in regard to Psalm 7, while adding some new observations based on a fully-Christian reading of the text. It is my sincere hope that this work will be presented for the glory of God, of which we are co-heirs with Christ,[2] and that those who study this work will be spiritually blessed.

Travis Mallett
Pullman, WA

For a more detailed analysis of the musical composition and to learn more about the author's work, please visit
www.travismallett.com.

---

[2]Romans 8:17

$$\overset{1}{\overbrace{\text{Vs. 1}}}|\overset{4}{\overbrace{\text{Vs. 2}}}|\overset{2}{\overbrace{\text{Vs. 3-5}}}|\overset{9}{\overbrace{\text{Vs. 6-7}}}|\overset{5}{\overbrace{\text{Vs. 8-9}}}\cdots$$

P_1	R_{10}	R_8	P_9	P_5
	I_4	I_2	I_9	I_5
			RI_3	R_{11}

$$|\overset{3}{\overbrace{\text{Vs. 10-13}}}|\overset{6}{\overbrace{\text{Vs. 14-16}}}|\overset{7}{\overbrace{\text{Vs. 17}}}$$

I_3	I_6	P_7
R_9		RI_1
RI_9		R_1
		I_7

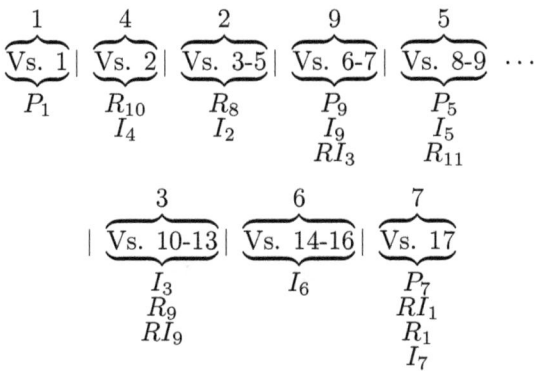

Figure 1: The musical composition uses a tone row to define both its macro- and micro-structures.

PSALM 7

A Shiggaion of David, which he sang to the Lord concerning the words of Cush, a Benjaminite.

¹ O Lord my God, in you do I take refuge; save me from all my pursuers and deliver me, ² lest like a lion they tear my soul apart, rending it in pieces, with none to deliver. ³ O Lord my God, if I have done this, if there is wrong in my hands, ⁴ if I have repaid my friend with evil or plundered my enemy without cause, ⁵ let the enemy pursue my soul and overtake it, and let him trample my life to the ground and lay my glory in the dust. *Selah* ⁶ Arise, O Lord, in your anger; lift yourself up against the fury of my enemies; awake for me; you have appointed a judgment. ⁷ Let the assembly of the peoples be gathered about you; over it return on high. ⁸ The Lord judges the peoples; judge me, O Lord, according to my righteousness and according to the integrity that is in me. ⁹ Oh, let the evil of the wicked come to an end, and may you establish the righteous—you who test the minds and hearts, O righteous God! ¹⁰ My shield is with God, who saves the upright in heart. ¹¹ God is a righteous judge, and a God who feels indignation every day. ¹² If a man does not repent, God will whet his sword; he has bent and readied his bow; ¹³ he has prepared for him his deadly weapons, making his arrows fiery shafts. ¹⁴ Behold, the wicked man conceives evil and is pregnant with mischief and gives birth to lies. ¹⁵ He makes a pit, digging it out, and falls into the hole that he has made. ¹⁶ His mischief returns upon his own head, and on his own skull his violence descends. ¹⁷ I will give to the Lord the thanks due to his righteousness, and I will sing praise to the name of the Lord, the Most High.

Introduction

Psalm 7 is a psalm of individual lament and a psalm of innocence[3] written by David, who has apparently been accused of vicious crimes, possibly high treason. David presents the situation before God, describing how he believes his accuser, if left unchecked, will tear him to pieces. David calls for God to descend upon the earth and rule with justice, vindicating the righteous and destroying the wicked. In the end, the evil deeds of the wicked recoil on himself and praise is directed to God, in what is not an atypical turn from distress to praise in the psalter. The psalm is titled with a mysterious superscription giving clues to its historical context. This commentary explores the historical context of Psalm 7, examines its structure and features, and provides a verse-by-verse commentary. The commentary concludes with reflections for the modern Christian.

Categories, Function, and Location

Category and Function

The genre of Psalm 7 has been difficult to determine since it contains elements of individual lament (verses 1–2), an oath (verses 3–5), a psalm of Yahweh's kingship (verses 6–12), and a thanksgiving hymn (verse 17).[4] The literature is remarkably divided on the categorization of this particular psalm. Some group Psalms 7 and 17 into a small category called the *psalms of innocence*[5] with the combined motifs of God's testing, imprecation, rejection of the way of the wicked, and submission to God.[6] Others create a larger grouping in which Psalms 7, 17, 109, and 139 are identified as *prayers of the accused*, representing a motif of violence. In both categories, the psalmists seek vindication from Yahweh,

---

[3] Jeffrey H. Tigay. "Psalm 7:5 and Ancient Near Eastern Treaties". In: *Journal of Biblical Literature* (1970), p. 178

[4] Willem A. VanGemeren. *Psalms*. Vol. 5. The Expositor's Bible Commentary. Grand Rapids, MI: Zondervan, 2008, p. 128

[5] Tigay, "Psalm 7:5 and Ancient Near Eastern Treaties", op. cit., p. 178

[6] Eric Peels. "'I Hate Them With Perfect Hatred' (Psalm 139:21–22)". In: *Tyndale Bulletin* 59.1 (2008), p. 44

because of charges made against them. They petition God for either their innocence to be declared[7] or their accusers to be judged guilty.[8] Because of David's vehement reaction against the accusers, some modern commentators include Psalm 7 in lists of imprecatory psalms.[9] Perhaps the most thoughtful categorization is that Psalm 7 is *formally an individual lament, of the psalm of innocence subcategory.*[10] In the individual lament, an individual worshipper cries out to Yahweh in his time of need. The structure of these psalms includes: an invocation of Yahweh; the complaint; the request for help; an expression of certainty that Yahweh will hear and answer the prayer; and a vow to offer a thanksgiving sacrifice. And this is a fitting description of the structure of Psalm 7.

Placement in the Psalter

The Book of Psalms is formally divided into five books, and it is often claimed that the organization and division of these five books corresponds to the structure and themes of the Pentateuch.[11] In keeping with this tradition, J. Vernon McGee offers the following outline of the First Book of Psalms which relates the psalms to accounts in Genesis which records man in a state of blessedness, fall, and recovery.[12]

McGee's outline of the First Book of Psalms is as follows:

1. Psalm 1: Perfect Man (last Adam)

2. Psalm 2: Rebellious Man

3. Psalm 3: Perfect Man rejected

---

[7]Deuteronomy 25:1

[8]D. G. Firth. "Responses to Violence in Some Lament Psalms of the Individual". In: *Skrif en Kerk* 17.2 (1996), p. 320

[9]J. Carl Laney. "A Fresh Look at the Imprecatory Psalms". In: *Bibliotheca Sacra* 138 (1981), p. 36; Peter White and M Th. "Causes for the upsurge of imprecatory prayer in contemporary African Christian churches". In: *American Journal of Biblical Theology* 13.32 (2012), p. 7

[10]Tigay, "Psalm 7:5 and Ancient Near Eastern Treaties", op. cit., p. 178

[11]Duane L Christensen. "The Book of Psalms Within the Canonical Process in Ancient Israel". In: *Journal-Evangelical Theological Society (JETS)* 39 (1996), p. 421

[12]J. Vernon McGee. *Poetry (Psalms 1-41)*. Vol. 17. Thru the Bible. Nashville, TN: Thomas Nelson, Inc., 1991

4. Psalm 4: Conflict between seed of Woman and Serpent

5. Psalm 5: Perfect Man in the midst of enemies

6. Psalm 6: Perfect Man in the midst of chastisement (bruising heel)

7. Psalm 7: Perfect Man in the midst of false witnesses

8. Psalm 8: Repair of Man comes through Man (bruising head)

9. Psalms 9–15: Enemy and Antichrist conflict; Final Deliverance

10. Psalms 16–41: Christ in the midst of His people, sanctifying them to God.

Since Psalms 1 and 2 are often cited as forming the introduction to the Book of Psalms, Psalm 7 is the conclusion to the first cluster of five psalms dealing with the "Perfect Man" theme.[13] According to this model, Psalm 7's place in the psalter is fitting as David asserts his innocence after being accused, i.e., David *is* a type of the Perfect Man in this instance. Additionally, the placement of Psalm 7 is important due to the importance of the number Seven in the text itself, as discussed later in this commentary.

Historical Context and Title

Psalm 7 is titled with the following superscription:

> A SHIGGAION OF DAVID, WHICH HE SANG TO THE
> LORD CONCERNING THE WORDS OF CUSH, A BEN-
> JAMINITE. (Psalm 7)

Psalms 3, 7, 18, 34, 51, 52, 54, 56, 57, 59, 60, 63, and 142 all have superscriptions which allude to an episode in the life of David. The titles of all these psalms is of a very consistent form and pattern. In all but two cases, these superscriptions evidence

---

[13]ibid., p. 3

an identical syntactical construction.[14] However, the superscriptions of both Psalms 7 and 18 differ somewhat from the others.[15] Specifically, the superscriptions of Psalms 7 and 18 do not relate unambiguously to any specific event in the life of David, as portrayed in the Deuteronomistic history. This stands in sharp contrast to every one of the other eleven syntactically identical titles.[16] On the basis of both syntax and function, it is concluded that the titles of Psalms 7 and 18 may not have been penned by the same hand as did the other superscriptions.[17]

While the other notations allow us to draw highly specific meanings from the context of history recorded outside the book of Psalms, what remains for Psalm 7 is an attempt to understand what content or context the author of the superscript intended it to add to a fuller understanding of the psalm. Unfortunately, we are given only two clues in the title of Psalm 7: the mention of "Cush, a Benjaminite" and the term *shiggaion.*

Cush, a Benjaminite

Much ink has been spilled over the mysterious reference to "Cush, a Benjaminite." However, despite the attempts of learned men, this person remains a mystery to this day, and virtually nothing is known about him. The problem stems from Cush making absolutely no appearance in any historical narrative.[18] Despite this, there are several popular theories on Cush's identity.

---

[14]For example, "A PSALM OF DAVID, WHEN HE FLED FROM ABSALOM HIS SON." (Psalm 3), "A PSALM OF DAVID, WHEN NATHAN THE PROPHET WENT TO HIM, AFTER HE HAD GONE IN TO BATHSHEBA." (Psalm 51), "A PSALM OF DAVID, WHEN HE WAS IN THE WILDERNESS OF JUDAH." (Psalm 63), and so on.

[15]Psalm 18 is titled, "A PSALM OF DAVID, THE SERVANT OF THE LORD, WHO ADDRESSED THE WORDS OF THIS SONG TO THE LORD ON THE DAY WHEN THE LORD DELIVERED HIM FROM THE HAND OF ALL HIS ENEMIES, AND FROM THE HAND OF SAUL."; Rodney R. Hutton. "Cush the Benjaminite and Psalm Midrash". In: *Hebrew Annual Review* 10 (1986), p. 123-124

[16]ibid., p. 124

[17]ibid., p. 126

[18]ibid., p. 126; Elwood Sylvester Berry. *Commentary on the Psalms: Psalms 1–50*. New York: Benziger Brothers, 1915, p. 74; Solomon B. Freehof. *The Jewish Commentary for Bible Readers*. Portland, OR: Union of American Hebrew Congregations, 1938, p. 24; Thomas L. Constable. *Notes on Psalms*. Garland: Sonic Light, 2015, p. 33

The most popular solutions have centered on taking the name "Cush" as a pseudonym for some more well-known person in history. Frequently-mentioned individuals are Shimei and Saul.[19]

Perhaps the oldest interpretation of this enigmatic passage is that "Cush" stands for King Saul.[20] We do not find, however, in the history of Saul that he "vomited forth any such words as these against David,"[21] as Martin Luther put it. Thus, this theory, although popular, generally has little evidence in its support.

A second theory is that the name "Cush" is possibly corruption or variation of "Kish", the name of the father of Saul. In 2 Samuel 16:5, Shimei is described as 'the son of Gera' (a remote ancestor), but his relationship to Kish is inferred from the genealogy of Mordecai, another Benjaminite, in Esther 2:5, where Mordecai is described as "the son of Jair, the son of Shimei, the son of Kish." Shimei, then, is here called by the name of his father Kish, and Kish is identified with the similarly named Cush for derogatory reasons, Cush being a son of Ham and the father of Nimrod, king of Babel and builder of Nineveh (Genesis 10:6–12).[22] Shimei, the Benjaminite is the one who cursed David when he was fleeing from Absalom.[23]

> [7] And Shimei said as he cursed, "Get out, get out, you man of blood, you worthless man! [8] The Lord has avenged on you all the blood of the house of Saul, in whose place you have reigned, and the Lord has given the kingdom into the hand of your son Absalom. See, your evil is on you, for you are a man of blood." (2 Samuel 16:7–8)

But David's response to Shimei in 2 Samuel 16:10–14, exhibits little of the emotional distress found in Psalm 7, for David is said to have merely continued on his way and "refreshed himself" when he arrived at his destination. The events surrounding Psalm 3 directly

---

[19]Hutton, "Cush the Benjaminite and Psalm Midrash", op. cit., p. 128

[20]ibid., p. 128

[21]Martin Luther. *Commentary on the First Twenty-Two Psalms*. London: Simpkin and R. Marshall, 1826, p. 335

[22]Roger T. Beckwith. "The Early History of the Psalter". In: *Tyndale Bulletin* 46.1 (1995), p. 19

[23]2 Samuel 16:5–14

precede the passage where Shimei curses David. In Psalm 3, David
pens a passionate prayer to God for deliverance from an immediate
physical threat. Psalm 7, on the other hand, is written in response
to some specific accusations, allegedly by Cush, and is primarily
concerned with *future* physical damages, or current psychological
distress; it seems unlikely that in the wake of imminent threat to
David's life (Psalm 3), Shimei's shouts from the road are of much
concern.

> *11 And David said to Abishai and to all his servants,*
> *"Behold, my own son seeks my life; how much more*
> *now may this Benjaminite! Leave him alone, and let*
> *him curse, for the Lord has told him to. 12 It may be*
> *that the Lord will look on the wrong done to me, and*
> *that the Lord will repay me with good for his cursing*
> *today." (2 Samuel 16:11–12)*

David's response to Shimei is quite optimistic, even dismissive.
Psalm 7, on the other hand, is obsessed with and emotionally dis-
traught about the wrongful accusations, and is likely written in
response to a different event.

Another interpretation is found as early as the Septuagint, when
there was an attempt to relate the superscription of Psalm 7 to a
person named "Cushi, the son of Yemeni."[24] In 2 Samuel 18:21–
32 it is related how a Cushite runner brought to David the news
of Absalom's death. If Psalm 7 was understood as a midrash on
the narrative of 2 Samuel 18–19, it was read as a declaration of
innocence, as David distanced himself from the treachery of Joab.
Here we have David's clear confession of innocence in the death of
his son, Absalom, and, at the same time, a statement of judgment
upon Joab for committing such treachery. We have displayed the
pathos and the anger of a man who has just lost his own son to
the arrogant insubordination of one of his most loyal friends, Joab,
who has now become his blood enemy.[25]

It is clear that none of the theories provide much compelling
direction for the historical context of Psalm 7. Despite good in-
tentions, much research, effort, and popular support of the above

---

[24]Hutton, "Cush the Benjaminite and Psalm Midrash", op. cit., p. 135
[25]ibid., p. 129

theories by commentators, this commentary recognizes that proceeding on incomplete conclusions is necessary.

Hence, the interpretation will be guided, but not defined, by the following observations:

1. Commentators generally date this psalm to the time of Absalom's rebellion, when the latent hostility of the Benjaminites resurged.[26]

2. The Benjaminites were, of course, King Saul's relatives who were hostile to David before and after David became king.[27]

3. The superscription simply says "a Benjaminite." Had he been well known, he would most probably have been called "*the* Benjaminite."[28]

4. Cush probably had, according to Psalm 7:4–5, only sought the friendship of David in order, when the opportunity came, all the more keenly to injure him—an occurrence quite in keeping with the character of those times.[29]

5. Regardless of the identity of Cush, Saul is likely the one against whom David is alleged to have committed a treachery, given the history between the two. This is a reasonable assumption shared by previous commentaries, which cast the psalm's interpretation within this context. For example, it is said that "In Psalm 7, David disavows any evil intention against Saul, a disavowal which he proves by refusing to take Saul's life when he had an easy opportunity to do so.[30] Additionally, the connection drawn between Psalm 7 and the David story is prompted by similarities to a wide range of interconnected narratives in 1 and 2 Samuel, all of which relate

---

[26] VanGemeren, *Psalms*, op. cit., p. 128

[27] Constable, *Notes on Psalms*, op. cit., p. 33

[28] Berry, *Commentary on the Psalms: Psalms 1–50*, op. cit., p. 74

[29] Heinrich Ewald. *Commentary on the Psalms*. Trans. by Edwin Johnson. Charleston, SC: BiblioBazaar, 2013, p. 74

[30] 1 Samuel 24; Freehof, *The Jewish Commentary for Bible Readers*, op. cit., p. 25

to David's restraint in his dealings with Saul and other Benjaminites.[31] Almost all commentaries concede this without further proof or discussion.

6. Although Saul may be the one whom David allegedly betrays, we do not find in the history of Saul that he ever made such accusations against David.[32] Thus, it is likely that if Saul is the object of the alleged treachery, then he is also *not* Cush the accuser.

It is not necessary to know the specific situation which prompted David to pen these words; neither is it necessary for us to understand precisely why the superscription exists. The general nature of the situation is evident from the text itself, especially in Psalm 7:3–5, and when combined with the human imagination, no technical answer to the question of the psalm's title is needed in order to enhance personal application. So often, it is difficult for the modern reader to relate to some of the events in the life of David, who underwent more tribulation than any modern student of the Word in a first-world setting may ever have to endure. The ambiguity of the superscript in this psalm may provide just enough information to produce an accurate interpretation, while leaving room for personal experiences to be considered. And perhaps the Holy Spirit, in His infinite knowledge, prompted the editor of the Psalms to pen the mysterious superscription, knowing that men who thirst for knowledge would search for the answer, and in doing so, perhaps one of them was, or will be, brought closer to the Lord and into a fuller understanding of His revelation and truths.

Shiggaion

The term *shiggaion* in the superscription is here also unknown. The ambiguity of the term is partially responsible for the difficulty in classifying Psalm 7 in a common category of psalms. Due to being described as a *shiggaion*, Psalm 7 has been explained variously as "stringed music," a "wandering" style, or as a "psalm of

---

[31]Yitzhak Berger. "The David–Benjaminite Conflict and the Intertextual Field of Psalm 7". In: *Journal for the Study of the Old Testament* 38.3 (2014), p. 279

[32]Luther, *Commentary on the First Twenty-Two Psalms*, op. cit., p. 335

lamentation."[33] Some take *shiggaion* to refer to an instrument of music; others believe it is probably a tune; still others claim it is the opening of a common chant of David.[34] The term is found in only one other place in Scripture (though in a plural form).[35] Habakkuk 3:1, which is attributed to a prophet of the late monarchy, is titled:

A PRAYER OF HABAKKUK THE PROPHET, ACCORDING TO SHIGIONOTH. (Habakkuk 3:1)

This prayer in Habakkuk ends with a note saying, "TO THE CHOIRMASTER: WITH STRINGED INSTRUMENTS."[36] Both the title and the final note are similar to the titles found in Psalms. Habakkuk's use of the musical interlude *Selah* (Habakkuk 3:3,9,13) also imitates the Davidic usage.[37] There are two common explanations of the term *shiggaion*:

1. The term *shiggaion* is a noun derived from a verb which means 'to err' or 'to wander.'[38] Some commentators presume an affinity with the Akkadian term *šegu* (to lament).[39] Although this noun occurs in only two places in Scripture, the verb from which it is derived is not uncommon, and is applied by Saul to his own errors with respect to David.[40]

2. Comparing the text of Psalm 7 and of Habakkuk 3, we note that neither is penitential. Therefore, it has been applied to the poetic form as being wild and ecstatic.[41]

---

[33] James W. Watts. "Psalmody in Prophecy: Habakkuk 3 in Context". In: *Forming Prophetic Literature: Essays on Isaiah and the Twelve in Honor of John D.W. Watts. Ed. James W. Watts and Paul R. House.* (1996), p. 211

[34] John Calvin. *Commentary on the Book Psalms.* Trans. by James Anderson. Vol. 3. Edinburgh: The Edinburgh Printing Company, 1847, p. 54

[35] Joseph Addison Alexander. *Commentary on Psalms.* Grand Rapids, MI: Kregel Publications, 1991, p. 41

[36] Habakkuk 3:19

[37] Beckwith, "The Early History of the Psalter", op. cit., p. 16

[38] Derek Kidner. *Psalms 1–72: An Introduction and Commentary.* Downers Grove, IL: InterVarsity Press, 1973, p. 52

[39] Artur Weiser. *The Psalms: A Commentary.* Trans. by Herbert Hartwell. Philadelphia: Westminster Press, 2000, p. 134

[40] 1 Samuel 26:1; Alexander, *Commentary on Psalms,* op. cit., p. 41

[41] Kidner, *Psalms 1–72: An Introduction and Commentary,* op. cit., p. 52

In both cases where the term is used, the idea of an erratic and excited text which wanders through multiple emotional landscapes is present.[42] Ewald suggests that it might be rendered, "a confused ode," a Dithyramb.[43] Finally, a more generic interpretation is that *shiggaion* simply means a poem with intense feeling.[44]

Structural Notes

Numerological Observations

The number Seven is an astonishingly important number in the Scriptures. From the seven days of creation[45] to the seven years of great plenty throughout all the land of Egypt[46] and subsequent seven years of famine[47] to the seven churches and seven spirits of God mentioned in Revelation, the number Seven was an almost tantalizing number to the authors of Scripture. In both Jewish and Christian traditions, seven signifies "totality of perfection" or "completeness."[48] There is thus a satisfying reason for this psalm's location in the psalter as the conclusion of the first cluster of five psalms dealing with "Perfect Man."[49] The location of Psalm 7 in the psalter was likely no accident, and too, the division of the verses into seventeen parts was probably not a chance occurrence.

Internally, Psalm 7 is the first psalm in which a pattern of seven uses of God's name is found. *Yahweh* begins it and *Yahweh* ends it, providing an inclusio to the whole. The name Yahweh appears a total of seven times in the poem, as does *Ĕl(ōhîm)*. If it be granted that *Ālāy* in Psalm 7:8 means "Most High" and that *Al-Elohim* in Psalm 7:10 means "The Most High God", then the divine

---

[42]Charles H. Spurgeon. *The Treasury of David*. Vol. 1. Peabody, MA: Hendrickson Publishers, 2011, p. 71

[43]A Dithyramb is a wild choral hymn of ancient Greece.

[44]Constable, *Notes on Psalms*, op. cit., p. 33

[45]Genesis 1

[46]Genesis 41:47

[47]Genesis 41:54

[48]Donald Senior and John J. Collins. *The Catholic Study Bible*. Oxford: Oxford University Press, 1990, pp. 398–399; Adele Berlin, Marc Zvi Brettler, et al. *The Jewish Study Bible: Jewish Publication Society Tanakh Translation*. Oxford: Oxford University Press, 2004, p. 382

[49]McGee, *Poetry (Psalms 1-41)*, op. cit., p. 3

appellation "Most High" appears three times (in three different forms) in the psalm, resulting in a total of seventeen (fourteen plus three or ten plus seven) occurrences of various divine names in all. The next psalm to employ one or more divine names seven times is Psalm 14.[50]

Structure and Outline

Each commentator has his own division of the psalm. The outline presented below is a modified version of Spurgeon's division.[51]

1. Psalm 7:1: Prayer Offered

2. Psalm 7:2: Danger Stated

3. Psalm 7:3–5: Oath of Innocence

4. Psalm 7:6–7: Plea for God to Arise to Judgment

5. Psalm 7:8–9: The Lord Hears

6. Psalm 7:10–13: Lord Clears His Servant and Threatens Wicked

7. Psalm 7:14–16: Slanderer Brings Curse on Himself

8. Psalm 7:17: Hymn of Praise

According to this division, Psalm 7:1–16 constitutes seven sections, while Psalm 7:17 is the final conclusion of the psalm. This division bears importance when considering the numerological observations.

Commentary on the Text

Verse 1: Prayer Offered

> O LORD *my God, in you do I take refuge; save me from all my pursuers and deliver me* ... (Psalm 7:1)

---

[50]Ronald Youngblood. "Divine Names in the Book of Psalms: Literary Structures and Number Patterns". In: *JANESCU* 19 (1989), pp. 177-178

[51]Spurgeon, *The Treasury of David*, op. cit.

The psalmist opens with a prayer for safety from his enemies. This is the first instance in the Psalms where David addresses the Almighty by the united names "Jehovah" and "my God".[52] In the opening phrase, David does three things at once.

1. He first affirms that Jehovah is his God. That is, that Jehovah is Lord over David. By uniting the names "Jehovah" and "God", David places particular emphasis on his addressee. Jehovah is not only his Lord and God, but he is the one that David turns to first and foremost in times of trouble.

2. With the phrase "in you do I take refuge," David, before even describing his problems, shows that he not only believes that God is the solution, but affirms that the battle is the Lord's.[53] Before the troubles have even hit, David is abiding in God.

3. Finally, David begins venting his troubles to none other than God, to whom he affirms his subservience. Whom better to lay our anguish before than the Almighty?

We should be mindful to follow David's example in our own lives. By seeking God's help, while always affirming His sovereignty, we rest in the knowledge that God will protect us. This does not mean that everything that troubles us will be automatically destroyed by our awesome God, but that God, in His sovereignty, as the psalmist affirms from the outset, "works for the good of those who love him, who have been called according to his purpose."[54]

Verse 2: Danger Stated

> ... *lest like a lion they tear my soul apart, rending it in pieces, with none to deliver.* (Psalm 7:2)

Both Psalms 7 and 17 make use of the simile of the lion[55] in

---

[52]ibid., p. 71

[53]1 Samuel 17:47; 2 Chronicles 20:15,17

[54]Romans 8:28

[55]It may be useful to study the use of lions in the Old Testament. The following list is taken from: Bob Utley. *Psalms: The Hymnal of Israel Book*

describing the actions of the enemy,[56] and thus seemingly speak of physical violence. However, the simile itself is applied to the accusation that has been made. This suggests, of course, that physical violence is a very real possibility, but at this stage it remains potential rather than actual. It is this potential for physical violence that causes the current distress, which is therefore psychological.[57] God hears our prayers, not only when we are suffering physical tragedies or are in some physical danger, but also when we are distressed about psychological matters. Of course, David, being close to the king, was very vulnerable to slander, and such accusations could cause great harm. It is possible he might, in a real and literal sense, be "rent to pieces," with no one to rescue him. If David had been captured, Saul could easily have him killed, or torn to pieces, with no rescuer in sight. We recall the imagery of Daniel in the lions' den, which admittedly is chronologically much later than this text. It was expected that Daniel would be torn to pieces by the lions, and no one in the land could rescue him, not even King Darius himself, for the law had been written. Daniel was saved, not by friends on earth, but by God, for when "Daniel was taken up out of the den, [...] no kind of harm was found on him, because

---

I. vol. 9B. Study Guide Commentary Series Old Testament. Marshall, TX: Bible Lessons International, 2012, p. 64. 1) Judah, Genesis 49:9; Micah 5:8, 2) YHWH on Israel's behalf, Numbers 24:9; Isaiah 31:4; Isaiah 35:9; Hosea 11:10, 3) Israel as a defeated lion, Ezekiel 19, 4) tribe of Dan, Deuteronomy 33:22, 5) David's power over lions, 1 Samuel 17:34–37, 6) Saul and Jonathan, 2 Samuel 1:23, 7) symbolic protectors of the throne of Solomon, 1 Kings 10:19–20, 8) God uses lions as punishment, 1 Kings 13:20; 2 Kings 17:25–26; Isaiah 10:19–20; metaphor in Job 4:10 and Jeremiah 2:30; Jeremiah 49:19,44; Lamentations 3:10; Amos 3:4,8,12; Amos 5:19; Hosea 5:14; Hosea 13:7–8; Nahum 2:11–12, 9) describe David's enemies from whom God will deliver, Psalm 7:2; Psalm 10:9; Psalm 17:12; Psalm 22:13,21, 10) a metaphor for unknown evil, Proverbs 22:13; Proverbs 26:13; Proverbs 28:15, 11) used to describe Babylon's military, Jeremiah 4:7; Jeremiah 49:19–22; Jeremiah 51:38, 12) the military of the nations against God's people, Jeremiah 5:6; Jeremiah 25:32–38; Jeremiah 50:17; Joel 1:6, 13) how God's people treat Him, Jeremiah 12:8, 14) how God's leaders treat the people, Ezekiel 22:25; Zephaniah 3:3, 15) metaphor for king's anger, Proverbs 19:12; Proverbs 20:2, 16) metaphor for the godly, Proverbs 28:1, 17) metaphor for the Messiah, Genesis 49:9; Revelation 5:5.

[56] Psalm 7:3; Psalm 17:12

[57] Firth, "Responses to Violence in Some Lament Psalms of the Individual", op. cit., pp. 320-321

he had trusted in his God."[58] Likewise, we find in the remainder of Psalm 7 that the vicious violence of David's enemies comes to naught because, like Daniel, David trusts in his God.

Verses 3–5: Oath of Innocence

> [3] O LORD my God, *if I have done this, if there is wrong in my hands,* [4] *if I have repaid my friend with evil or plundered my enemy without cause,* [5] *let the enemy pursue my soul and overtake it, and let him trample my life to the ground and lay my glory in the dust.* Selah (Psalm 7:3–5)

In these verses, David protests his innocence with a deprecatory oath.[59] It is here that we find out what the alleged crime was, but only inferentially from the oath in which David denies wrongdoing. This type of oath is common in the Psalms and usually takes the form: "If I have done any such thing—if I ever behaved like so-and-so, then let so-and-so tread my life down upon the earth." Given God's well-documented role in vindication,[60] this reaction is not unprecedented.

C. S. Lewis warns that "all this of course has its spiritual danger. It leads into that typically Jewish prison of self-righteousness which Our Lord so often terribly rebuked."[61] Of course there is some danger in constantly asserting that you are right in a situation. The embarrassment of strongly claiming that we are in the right, only to be proved wrong at some point, can be avoided if we exhibit some humility. We must be careful to avoid the fate of the fool spoken of in Proverbs 26:12: "Do you see a person wise in their own eyes? There is more hope for a fool than for them." We can complement this notion of avoiding the folly of leaning on our own

---

[58] Daniel 6:23

[59] Berry, *Commentary on the Psalms: Psalms 1–50*, op. cit., p. 75

[60] Malachi 4:3; Zechariah 10:5; Habakkuk 3:13; Jeremiah 17:13; Isaiah 63:3; Isaiah 10:6; Psalm 60:12; Psalm 49:12; Psalm 44:5; Job 31:5–10; Job 40:12; Revelation 14:20; Psalm 37:38; Proverbs 14:11; Psalm 94:23; Psalm 28:5; Psalm 73:19; Psalm 92:7; 2 Peter 3:6; Romans 9:22; 2 Thessalonians 1:9

[61] C. S. Lewis. *Reflections on the Psalms.* New York: Harcourt, Inc., 1956, p. 17

understanding[62] by following the instructions of Micah 6:8: "And what does the Lord require of you but to do justice, and to love kindness, and to walk humbly with your God?"

But "to do justice" is what the psalmist is referring to here. There are times when we *are* in the right about the situation. In the case of David being accused of treachery against Saul, David *was*, in fact, without fault. David never manifested any animosity against Saul. On the contrary, he exhibited his respectful relationship to the king of Israel to a remarkable degree.[63] Perhaps we know we have acted justly, or have been robbed of credit rightfully due to us, or accused of something we haven't done. It is easy to recall or imagine the indignation that rises up in us when we are wrongfully treated.

David's oath of innocence teaches us a few things: first, he has been wrongfully treated, and rather than spending time and energy defending himself before men, he takes his oaths of innocence directly to God. Second, David is obviously distressed in this psalm. We understand the inner turmoil and the emotional anguish. This is an excellent example that should encourage us *never* to treat another person unfairly. That is, we wish never to inflict such emotional anguish upon our fellow beings, and hence we should be careful to guard our ways and interactions with others to ensure that no loose comment hints even slightly of accusation that may not be true. For even if the smallest whiff of accusation is directed towards us, very strong emotions can surge, perhaps disproportionately more severe than the initial accusation warrants. Thus, we have here an example of how we can react to accusations against us, viz., by bringing our fears to God, and we also find a strong warning against accusing falsely or acting unjustly

Verses 6–7: Plead for God to Arise to Judgment

> [6] *Arise, O* LORD, *in your anger; lift yourself up against the fury of my enemies; awake for me; you have appointed a judgment.* [7] *Let the assembly of the peoples*

---

[62]Proverbs 3:5

[63]George Phillips. *A Commentary on the Psalms*. Vol. 2. London: Williams and Norgate, 1872, p. 89-90

be gathered about you; over it return on high. (Psalm
7:6–7)

Here the psalmist, in the wake of injustice, requests that the
Lord rise up against his enemies and rule over "the assembly of
the peoples." In the psalmist's eyes, this sort of ruling is not the
oppressive tyrannical rule we might imagine today. Rather, it is
the image of the Lord judging rightly in civil cases. Some commentators suggest that this passage has more earthly consequences in
David's life. They propose that David is promising that as soon as
he becomes ruler of the kingdom, he will endeavor that justice will
be the norm. Under Saul, religion may have been disregarded, or
such a recklessness in iniquity prevailed, that few or none sought
God.[64] However, in Psalm 7:8, where David asks to be judged according to his integrity, it is made clear that this is truly a hope
for a literal vindication from the Lord.

Verses 8–9: The Lord Hears

> [8] *The* LORD *judges the peoples; judge me, O* LORD,
> *according to my righteousness and according to the in-*
> *tegrity that is in me.* [9] *Oh, let the evil of the wicked*
> *come to an end, and may you establish the righteous—*
> *you who test the minds and hearts, O righteous God!*
> (Psalm 7:8–9)

Taken out of context, Psalm 7:8 can cause some confusion. Con-
trasting David's statement, "...judge me, O Lord, according to my
righteousness and according to the integrity that is in me" with
other passages which assert that "...there is no one on earth who
is righteous, no one who does what is right and never sins,"[65] reveals an apparent contradiction. How could David request that he
be judged according to his righteousness, when elsewhere it is af-
firmed that no one is righteous? Clearly the transition from being
innocent of wrongdoing in the particular situation (Psalm 7:3–5) to
requesting God literally judge him according to his righteousness
in Psalm 7:9 requires some thoughtful reflection.

---

[64]Calvin, *Commentary on the Book Psalms*, op. cit., p. 59
[65]Ecclesiastes 7:20

Here are three interpretations:

1. It is absolutely critical that Psalm 7:8 be interpreted in light of Psalm 7:3–5. The psalmist is not claiming sinlessness, but that he had not done what he was accused of doing![66] All such expressions of innocence are qualified by the confession of unworthiness in Psalm 6 and elsewhere, which sufficiently demonstrate that the Psalmist makes no claim to absolute perfection and innocence, nor to any righteousness independent of God's sovereign mercy.[67]

2. From the Christian perspective, this may be rectified by a logical argument: David is spoken of in the "Faith Chapter" (Hebrews 11:32), where the patriarchs are said to have accomplished great things and achieved salvation by faith and not by their own righteousness. We also learn in 1 Corinthians 1:30 that "because of [God][68] you are in Christ Jesus, who became to us wisdom from God, righteousness and sanctification and redemption." We who are in Christ Jesus *do* possess a true and pure righteousness given from God. By the implicit indication in Hebrews, David "became an heir of the righteousness that comes by faith."[69] Without this clarification, it is folly to assert our innocence before God, who is pure and holy. But with a cloak of righteousness,[70] which is Christ Jesus, we will stand confidently before the Lord on the day of judgment.[71] As one commentator explained:

> *We may plead "not guilty" before men when we cannot thus plead before God. Job vindicated himself before his friends, but in the presence of God abased himself, and repented in sackcloth and ashes. We may often most properly assert our*

---

[66]Utley, *Psalms: The Hymnal of Israel Book I*, op. cit., p. 67; Kidner, *Psalms 1–72: An Introduction and Commentary*, op. cit., p. 81

[67]Alexander, *Commentary on Psalms*, op. cit., p. 43

[68]1 Corinthians 1:29

[69]Hebrews 11:7

[70]Job 29:14; Revelation 19:8; Isaiah 61:10; Isaiah 59:17; Isaiah 11:5; Psalm 132:9; Zechariah 3:4; Revelation 3:4

[71]1 John 4:17; 1 John 2:28

integrity before men, but "concerning the law of
our God," it is another thing. We may plead "not
guilty" before God when we have rested in the mer-
its of Christ.[72]

3. Finally, David may be here prophetically uttering the voice
of Christ. David is considered a *type* of Christ, and there are
many obvious parallels between the two.[73] This psalm may
be a foreshadowing of Jesus' own words regarding the San-
hedrin trial where he was accused of blasphemy. "If I have
done this, if there is wrong in my hands"[74] and "judge me,
O LORD, according to my righteousness and according to the
integrity that is in me"[75] sound more natural in an ultimate
spiritual sense from the mouth of Jesus than from David.
This, of course, is how Jesus defends us before the Father on
the Day of Judgment. When the accuser brings up our sins
before the Almighty and demands that we be punished ac-
cordingly, Jesus, his righteousness cloaking us from the start
of the trial, steps in and states that, if the accused, who has
placed faith in Him, is indeed guilty, then "trample my life
to the ground and lay my glory in the dust."[76] David offers
the oath of innocence based on his faith that the promised
Messiah would become "sin who knew no sin, so that in him
we might become the righteousness of God."[77] That is, that
Christ would suffer the tragedy of being ripped to pieces[78] by
the wrath of the Father "with none to deliver"[79] to appease
the judicial requirements for the sin that was committed.

The last request here is that God will "let the evil of the wicked

---

[72]W. L. Watkinson. *The Preacher's Commentary on the Book of Psalms*.
Vol. 1. The Preacher's Complete Homiletical Commentary on the Old Testament. London: Richard D. Dickinson, 1881, p. 24

[73]Psalm 2; Joseph Samuel C. F. Frey. *Course of Lectures on the Scripture
Types*. New York: D. Fanshaw, 1841, p. 195

[74]Psalm 7:3

[75]Psalm 7:8

[76]Psalm 7:5

[77]2 Corinthians 5:21

[78]Psalm 7:2

[79]Psalm 7:2

come to an end, and [...] establish the righteous."[80] A major purpose of the judgments against evildoers in the imprecatory psalms is to establish the righteous. As God judges the wicked, He is also invoked to establish the righteous.[81] The Lord ruling over the peoples, making right the wrongs committed against us, is the sort of judgment to look forward to, not dread. And as Christians, we can look forward to the Day of Judgment with eagerness when all the wrong in the world will be righted and our own sinfulness, being covered by the blood of Christ, will be vanquished in the final act of sanctification.

Verses 10–13: The Lord's Response

10 My shield is with God, who saves the upright in heart.
11 God is a righteous judge, and a God who feels indignation every day. 12 If a man does not repent, God will whet his sword; he has bent and readied his bow; 13 he has prepared for him his deadly weapons, making his arrows fiery shafts. (Psalm 7:10–13)

The psalmist now returns to his opening statement which claims that God is his refuge. God is here described as being a "shield [...] who saves the upright in heart."[82] The word "shield" is taken from the ancient battlefield and is a common metaphor in the psalms for God's defense of His own people.[83] The word was first spoken by God to Abram in Genesis 15:1 where the Lord came to Abram in a vision and said,[84] "Fear not, Abram, I am your shield; your reward shall be very great" (Genesis 15:1). Later, in Genesis 15:6, it is said that Abram "believed the LORD, and he counted it to him as righteousness." Here we have some further support that David's reference to "my righteousness" in Psalm 7:8 is not founded in the sort of self-righteousness that brings about death, but defined by the righteousness that comes by faith.

---

[80]Psalm 7:9

[81]Laney, "A Fresh Look at the Imprecatory Psalms", op. cit., p. 41

[82]Psalm 7:10

[83]Psalm 7:10; Psalm 18:30; Psalm 28:7; Psalm 33:20; Psalm 59:11; Psalm 84:9,11; Psalm 115:9–11; Psalm 119:114; Psalm 144:2

[84]J. Vernon McGee. *Psalm 119: A Commentary Outline—The Golden ABC's of the Word of God.* Kansas City, MO: Word of Truth, 2009, p. 60

In Psalm 7:11, God is described as "a righteous judge, and a God who feels indignation every day." That is, the Divine punishment for evil never relaxes unless men repent.[85] This is evidenced by the conditional statement, "if a man does not repent," which reveals that God waits for repentance when he seems merely dilatory.[86] When God appears to delay the judgment of evil people, He is actually waiting for them to repent. However, God also "whets his sword; . . . and readies his bow; and prepares for him his deadly weapons,"[87] so that if they do *not* repent, God will surely deal justice.

Since God expresses his indignation every day, and on account of the "every day,"[88] God's behavior is certainly not restricted to the enemies of David.[89] Rather, God is angry about *all* those who walk in paths of unrighteousness. Some may think that David is calling God's wrath down upon only those who have hurt David personally. While this is true to some extent, the previous imagery of God ruling over "the assembly of the peoples"[90] indicates that God's interests are both broad and detailed. That is, that God is concerned with capturing the hearts of nations as well as individuals.

Verses 14–16: Slanderer Brings Curse on Himself

14 Behold, the wicked man conceives evil and is pregnant with mischief and gives birth to lies. 15 He makes a pit, digging it out, and falls into the hole that he has made. 16 His mischief returns upon his own head, and on his own skull his violence descends. (Psalm 7:14–16)

The psalmist here fantasizes about his enemies coming to ruin through natural consequences, and expresses a worldview wisdom in which the sin of false accusation inevitably recoils back on the

---

[85] Psalm 7:11–12; Freehof, *The Jewish Commentary for Bible Readers*, op. cit., p. 26

[86] Kidner, *Psalms 1–72: An Introduction and Commentary*, op. cit., p. 81

[87] Psalm 7:12–13

[88] Psalm 7:11

[89] E. W. Hengstenberg. *Commentary on Psalms*. London: John Robertson and Co., 1863, p. 120

[90] Psalm 7:7

accuser. The violence that has been experienced by David in this
case is primarily psychological. Yet the punishment that is desired
is described in physical terms. This, however, is not an unfair
request in light of the law of false accusation found in Deuteronomy
19:16–21.[91] The justice system recorded by Moses differs greatly
to the system used in Western cultures today. When a person
was accused of a crime, the evidence presented against him was
usually submitted by witnesses. The majority of the trial was spent
determining the credibility and character of the witness. If the
witness was credible, then the accused would be found guilty of
the crime according to the witness's testimony. To modern ears,
this system may sound prone to error and injustice. Ideally, the
accused are presumed innocent until absolutely, beyond a shadow of
a doubt, proved guilty. In modern-day courts, eye-witness accounts
are often rejected because they are deemed unreliable. However,
the Mosaic Law was designed to reduce the probability of injustice
due to false accusations by making the punishment for perjury so
severe as to discourage anyone from even considering committing
perjury.

> *[18] The judges shall inquire diligently, and if the witness
> is a false witness and has accused his brother falsely,
> [19] then you shall do to him as he had meant to do to his
> brother. So you shall purge the evil from your midst.
> [20] And the rest shall hear and fear, and shall never
> again commit any such evil among you. [21] Your eye
> shall not pity. It shall be life for life, eye for eye, tooth
> for tooth, hand for hand, foot for foot.* (Deuteronomy
> 19:18–21)

This judicial system had the benefit of being able to swiftly
deal justice while being effective at reducing injustice. Today, we
see justice taking years or even decades to be imparted, requiring
great expense; and too often, justice isn't served at all. Thus, when
David in Psalm 7 wishes that the slanderer's "violence comes down
on his own head," when the actual harm to David at this point is

---

[91]Firth, "Responses to Violence in Some Lament Psalms of the Individual",
op. cit., pp. 321

only a future *possibility*, we can understand this as fair per the ancient justice system.

Furthermore, in Psalm 7:15–16, we see that God had prepared his deadly weapons, bent his bow and sharpened his sword. But here, in the spiritual sense, it is understood that man causes these acts to himself.[92] As one commentator put it, "All sin is the digging of a pit."[93] And we can expect the consequences for our actions to recoil on us. The God of moral law is also the same God who created the laws of nature. And just as the laws of nature are modeled precisely as a series of actions and reactions, that is, that the universe is *causal*, we can expect our actions to also have consequences from which we cannot hide. Thus, we should think carefully about the consequences of what we are about to do lest they recoil on ourselves.

Verse 17: Hymn of Praise

> [17] *I will give to the* LORD *the thanks due to his righteousness, and I will sing praise to the name of the* LORD, *the Most High.* (Psalm 7:17)

The final stanza of this psalm is a hymn of praise. This verse was likely sung as a chorus by the people.[94] The words "I will sing praise to the name of the LORD, the Most High," is the exact phrase repeated in Psalm 9:2 and Psalm 92:1.[95] "The Most High" is a title seldom found outside the Psalms, but first encountered in the story of Melchizedek and Abram.[96] It is especially appropriate that the last word in this psalm announces in faith, as an ever-present fact, the exaltation which Psalm 7:6 longs to see proclaimed in power.[97]

---

[92]Emanuel Swedenborg. *Commentary on the Psalms.* Boston: The Massachusetts New-Church Union, 1910, p. 23

[93]Watkinson, *The Preacher's Commentary on the Book of Psalms*, op. cit., p. 27

[94]Berry, *Commentary on the Psalms: Psalms 1–50*, op. cit., p. 78

[95]Utley, *Psalms: The Hymnal of Israel Book I*, op. cit., p. 71

[96]The Dead Sea Scrolls document 11Q13 holds that Melchizedek was an angel or "a godlike being" who was part of the Divine Council referred to in Psalm 82:1 and Psalm 7:7–8; David Sielaff. *Who Was Melchizedek?* 2011. URL: http://www.askelm.com/doctrine/d110101.pdf (visited on 07/07/2020).

[97]Kidner, *Psalms 1–72: An Introduction and Commentary*, op. cit., p. 82

Just as the opening to Psalm 7 affirms God's protection before
the problem is even stated, the ending of the psalm also presents
a statement of God's faithfulness to deliver us. It is not insignif-
icant that after asking to be judged by "my righteousness," the
psalmist ends his prayer with praise for *God's* righteousness. For
the Christian, these are one and the same, *by faith*. Spurgeon
quotes William Dyer in regard to Psalm 7:17 in a very fitting sum-
mary of the essence of this final hymn of praise:

> *To bless God for mercies is the way to increase them;*
> *to bless him for miseries is the way to remove them: no*
> *good lives so long as that which is thankfully improved;*
> *no evil dies so soon as that which is patiently endured.*[98]

Summary and Reflections

Can the contemporary Christian sing the words of Psalm 7 with
enthusiasm and with a true heart of worship? Absolutely. In fact,
Luther, in "A Simple Way to Pray" places "Make their wicked
schemes, tricks, and devices to come to nothing so that these may
be turned against them, as we sing in Psalm 7" under the petition,
"Your will be done, on earth as it is in heaven."[99] That is, the
prayer of Psalm 7 is an exposition of "Your will be done, on earth
as it is in heaven."[100] As Christians who are in the world, but
not *of* the world, we look upon the state of wickedness in the
world and cry to God for the wrong to become right, the wicked to
repent or be punished, and the righteous to be vindicated. One of
God's functions as Judge is to vindicate the righteous and condemn
the guilty. David calls on God to do so in his case. To vindicate
means to show a righteous person to be righteous when others have
accused him or her of being wicked. It is fitting for God to establish
the righteous and to destroy the wicked because He is righteous
Himself.[101] The curses against the wicked in Psalm 7 double as

---

[98]Spurgeon, *The Treasury of David*, op. cit., p. 77
[99]Matthew 6:10; Martin Luther. *A Simple Way to Pray*. Louisville, KY:
Westminster John Knox Press, 2000, p. 2
[100]Matthew 6:10
[101]Constable, *Notes on Psalms*, op. cit., p. 34

blessings for the righteous. For as the wicked are diminished, the righteous are established.

David also spends time reflecting on God's character. Reflection on God's character and ways of working encourages God's people to trust in Him and praise Him when experiencing injustice and hostility from the wicked.[102] This song is a splendid example of the manner in which, even in extreme danger and unrest, higher contemplation yields true hope and rest, pacifying the storm of the passions.[103]

Finally, in each of the *psalms of innocence* the psalmists do not seek permission from Yahweh to carry out such violence personally. Instead, the petitions leave the final decision to Yahweh. Psalm 7 assumes that Yahweh brings justice, and thus there is no need to ask permission to go further. The other three *prayers of the accused* do ask for more, but always in submission to Yahweh.[104] We are not called to take vengeance into our own hands, and, no matter how much we wish we could, God is ultimately in control. Even if we cannot understand all His reasons for delaying judgment to the wicked who cause pain in this world, we know that God is waiting for them to repent. If we reflect on our own lives, we find evidence that God is patient with us as well. Thus, the Lord deserves glory and our gratitude.

---

[102]ibid., p. 35

[103]Ewald, *Commentary on the Psalms*, op. cit., p. 76

[104]Firth, "Responses to Violence in Some Lament Psalms of the Individual", op. cit., pp. 321-322; Laney, "A Fresh Look at the Imprecatory Psalms", op. cit., p. 42

BIBLIOGRAPHY

Alexander, Joseph Addison. *Commentary on Psalms*. Grand Rapids, MI: Kregel Publications, 1991.

Beckwith, Roger T. "The Early History of the Psalter". In: *Tyndale Bulletin* 46.1 (1995), pp. 1–27.

Berger, Yitzhak. "The David–Benjaminite Conflict and the Intertextual Field of Psalm 7". In: *Journal for the Study of the Old Testament* 38.3 (2014), pp. 279–296.

Berlin, Adele, Marc Zvi Brettler, et al. *The Jewish Study Bible: Jewish Publication Society Tanakh Translation*. Oxford: Oxford University Press, 2004.

Berry, Elwood Sylvester. *Commentary on the Psalms: Psalms 1–50*. New York: Benziger Brothers, 1915.

Calvin, John. *Commentary on the Book Psalms*. Trans. by James Anderson. Vol. 3. Edinburgh: The Edinburgh Printing Company, 1847.

Christensen, Duane L. "The Book of Psalms Within the Canonical Process in Ancient Israel". In: *Journal-Evangelical Theological Society (JETS)* 39 (1996), pp. 421–432.

Constable, Thomas L. *Notes on Psalms*. Garland: Sonic Light, 2015.

Ewald, Heinrich. *Commentary on the Psalms*. Trans. by Edwin Johnson. Charleston, SC: BiblioBazaar, 2013.

Firth, D. G. "Responses to Violence in Some Lament Psalms of the Individual". In: *Skrif en Kerk* 17.2 (1996), pp. 317–328.

Freehof, Solomon B. *The Jewish Commentary for Bible Readers*. Portland, OR: Union of American Hebrew Congregations, 1938.

Frey, Joseph Samuel C. F. *Course of Lectures on the Scripture Types*. New York: D. Fanshaw, 1841.

Hengstenberg, E. W. *Commentary on Psalms*. London: John Robertson and Co., 1863.

Hutton, Rodney R. "Cush the Benjaminite and Psalm Midrash". In: *Hebrew Annual Review* 10 (1986), pp. 123–137.

Kidner, Derek. *Psalms 1–72: An Introduction and Commentary*. Downers Grove, IL: InterVarsity Press, 1973.

Laney, J. Carl. "A Fresh Look at the Imprecatory Psalms". In: *Bibliotheca Sacra* 138 (1981), pp. 35–45.

Lewis, C. S. *Reflections on the Psalms*. New York: Harcourt, Inc., 1956.

Luther, Martin. *A Simple Way to Pray*. Louisville, KY: Westminster John Knox Press, 2000.

— *Commentary on the First Twenty-Two Psalms*. London: Simpkin and R. Marshall, 1826.

McGee, J. Vernon. *Poetry (Psalms 1-41)*. Vol. 17. Thru the Bible. Nashville, TN: Thomas Nelson, Inc., 1991.

— *Psalm 119: A Commentary Outline—The Golden ABC's of the Word of God*. Kansas City, MO: Word of Truth, 2009.

Peels, Eric. "'I Hate Them With Perfect Hatred' (Psalm 139:21–22)". In: *Tyndale Bulletin* 59.1 (2008), pp. 35–51.

Phillips, George. *A Commentary on the Psalms*. Vol. 2. London: Williams and Norgate, 1872.

Senior, Donald and John J. Collins. *The Catholic Study Bible*. Oxford: Oxford University Press, 1990.

Sielaff, David. *Who Was Melchizedek?* 2011. URL: http://www.askelm.com/doctrine/d110101.pdf (visited on 07/07/2020).

Spurgeon, Charles H. *The Treasury of David*. Vol. 1. Peabody, MA: Hendrickson Publishers, 2011.

Swedenborg, Emanuel. *Commentary on the Psalms*. Boston: The Massachusetts New-Church Union, 1910.

Tigay, Jeffrey H. "Psalm 7:5 and Ancient Near Eastern Treaties". In: *Journal of Biblical Literature* (1970), pp. 178–186.

Utley, Bob. *Psalms: The Hymnal of Israel Book I*. Vol. 9B. Study Guide Commentary Series Old Testament. Marshall, TX: Bible Lessons International, 2012.

VanGemeren, Willem A. *Psalms*. Vol. 5. The Expositor's Bible Commentary. Grand Rapids, MI: Zondervan, 2008.

Watkinson, W. L. *The Preacher's Commentary on the Book of Psalms*. Vol. 1. The Preacher's Complete Homiletical Commentary on the Old Testament. London: Richard D. Dickinson, 1881.

Watts, James W. "Psalmody in Prophecy: Habakkuk 3 in Context". In: *Forming Prophetic Literature: Essays on Isaiah and the Twelve in Honor of John D.W. Watts. Ed. James W. Watts and Paul R. House*. (1996), pp. 209–223.

Weiser, Artur. *The Psalms: A Commentary*. Trans. by Herbert Hartwell. Philadelphia: Westminster Press, 2000.

White, Peter and M Th. "Causes for the upsurge of imprecatory prayer in contemporary African Christian churches". In: *American Journal of Biblical Theology* 13.32 (2012), p. 5.

Youngblood, Ronald. "Divine Names in the Book of Psalms: Literary Structures and Number Patterns". In: *JANESCU* 19 (1989), pp. 171–181.

SCRIPTURE INDEX

31

NOTES

US $19.95   Biblical Criticism & Interpretation/OT

ISBN 978-1-953516-00-8   (hardcover)

5 1 9 9 5

9 781953 516008

www.vorstossen.com

Made in the USA
Imprint: Lulu.com

www.ingramcontent.com/pod-product-compliance
Lightning Source LLC
Chambersburg PA
CBHW070828100426
42813CB00003B/530